Unsheathed:

24 Contemporary Poets Take Up the Knife

Edited by Betsy Mars

Unsheathed: 24 Contemporary Poets Take Up the Knife

© Copyright 2019 Betsy Mars/Kingly Street Press
All rights reserved. No portion of this book may be used or reproduced in any manner whatsoever without written permission of the author or the publisher, except in the case of credited epigraphs or brief quotations embedded in articles or reviews.

Editor-in-Chief
Betsy Mars

Proofreader
Daniel Naphas

Front Cover Art
Lorette C. Luzajic, "Cut to the Chase"

Kingly Street Press Logo Design
Kat Naphas

Kingly Street Press
www.kinglystreetpress.com

First Edition
Printed in the United States of America

ISBN-13: 978-1-7333927-0-9

Table of Contents

*In the beginning there was the word, or in this case, the sentence: **"Knives cut both bread and throats."***

Introduction
Marc Alan Di Martino/Betsy Mars

Alts Drait Zich Arum Broit Un Toit
Jay Brecker
11

Duality
Marc Alan Di Martino
12

Domestic Violence
Alexis Rhone Fancher
13

Slather
Brian Harman
14

A Vampirical Sonnet
Stephen Howarth
16

Explanation
Sean Kelbley
17

My Uncle of Alcohol
Judy Kronenfeld
19

Instructions for Cutting
Juliet Latham
21

Love, God, Murder
Lorette C. Luzajic
24

Duality
Betsy Mars
27

The Paper Cut of Dreams
Michael Minassian
28

Goat
Penelope Moffet
29

Uses of the Knife: Dario Cecchini
Robbi Nester
31

These Lines Draw Mountains
Cristina M.R. Norcross
32

Black Lace Surrender
Shannon Phillips
33

He Pleads the Fifth
Jeannie E. Roberts
35

Bread and Throats
Sarah Russell
36

If This Be Progress (An Acrostic)
Kenneth Salzmann
37

Double-edged
Jeff Santosuossa
39

The Blade Itself
Ryan Stone
40

Assassin
Brent Terry
41

Knife Sonnet
Alexandra Umlas
43

The Impalement Arts
Alan Walowitz
44

Poetry Class, Circa 1998
Julie Weiss
46

Acknowledgements

Author Biographies

Introduction

Marc: Betsy Mars has asked me to write a short introduction to *Unsheathed*. Here are the facts as I remember them. Betsy and I—who have never met in person—were discussing the pros and cons of social media. Apropos I wrote, Knives cut both bread and throats. "Is that an Italian saying?" she inquired. I said no, it's just me coming up with things out of the blue, maybe the first line of a future poem. Riffing. Shpritzing. Five minutes later she sent her own poem with that first line—throwing down the gauntlet, so to speak. I took another five to send her mine. She replied—or maybe I suggested—that it might be fun to see what others would do with the line. In a matter of days she'd gotten out the word to a number of other poets, and we decided it would be fun to gather the results in an anthology. I sent out three or four invitations of my own, divesting myself of any further responsibility and leaving the editorial work to Betsy, whose enthusiasm for the project was evident. What she did with it you now hold in your hands.

Betsy: I remember it as follows. Early one Sunday morning I woke up and exchanged messages with Marc about a reading I had attended the previous night. Marc had an upcoming reading with one of the poets in Rome. We discussed the pros and cons of social media, and then Marc responded with the obviously brilliant line about knives.

I greedily asked "What is that? Some Italian saying?" He told me it was the first line of a poem.
I replied "Damn. I wanted to steal it."
Marc offered to make an exchange. A line for a line.
I panicked, went blank, and told him it was too much pressure.
I knew I couldn't come up with anything comparable. Or, in

that moment *anything*, period.

So, he told me I could just take it and play with it, and, as I intended to drift back to sleep, I jotted down the line.

Which led to another, and soon I had a poem that I kind of liked and I eagerly asked Marc if I could share it with him, hoping he would think it was okay. Or would kindly lie and tell me he did.

He then took it on, outdid me, and as we began to realize the potential variety that that single line could produce, Marc said we could maybe see if others were interested and create an e-book. Not being a realist and suffering from sleep deprivation and a kind of poetry-induced mania, I suggested that maybe I could create an actual book. This is the point where Marc, in his sanity and generosity, turned it over to me.

I reached out to as many people as I could, given the limits of time and an awakening realization that maybe I was out of my depth. Soon, these poems came rolling in.

Initially, poets adhered to the instruction to use it as a first line. Then the scofflaws arrived.

I started to receive some that used the line in the middle or at the end of the poem. I loved the poems and decided that that was alright, as long as the line was in the poem.

Then came the real deviants who chopped up the line, pared it down, scattered it like breadcrumbs throughout the poem. I wanted to take them by the throat, but a wise friend said that I could view the line as a prompt, like the image for an ekphrastic work, and see the poems as responses to that prompt. So, I again evolved in my thinking, and decided to re-sheath my Exacto blade. Besides, they were pretty brilliant pieces, and so they made the cut.

It has been an honor to be entrusted first by Marc, and then by this wide-ranging, far-flung group of writers who gifted this first-time publisher their remarkable poems.

I hope you enjoy them as much as I do.

Jay Becker

Alts Drait Zich Arum Broit Un Toit

Everything revolves around bread and death
               —A Yiddish Proverb

The past—that racy, self-aware
jokester—will return; it always does.

Embedded on a mission to explore
an urgency of desire, after trading
sweaters—Icelandic for Swedish—

I tell a man whose name I won't remember
of the love I have for him, a dangerous
euphoria of takeoffs or landings.

A siren tones down to hum and sing—
the sound of his own searching. And soon
the room feels cold, underwater—

imagine the North or Baltic Seas—as just
outside my window the Pacific could be
seen slicing back and forth; beyond us

the last crust of sun penetrates
the horizon as we sit at the table,
the remains of a meal between us.

It takes what it takes to end something.
Like knives cut both bread and throats.

Marc Alan Di Martino

Duality

Knives cut both bread and throats
tongues and fruit, a length of rope
to fashion both knot and noose.
A blade can scissor hope,
whittle back bone, crack
skull, scrape out the pulp
from teeth then sign its name
in flesh soft as an apricot.
It is a weapon, and is not.

Alexis Rhone Fancher

Domestic Violence

Knives cut both bread and throats, he warns, the stiletto's steel tip teasing my trachea. A love tap. I'm used to it. I don't react anymore; I bake. I knead, pound the dough instead of him. Each day when he leaves for court, those $2,000 suits camouflaging his viciousness, a brief reprieve. I envision his face in the smacked-down dough, push out the air pockets, dream of suffocation. I slap him, punch him, only to watch him rise. While he proofs, I look for loopholes, binge-watch *Forensic Files*, its endless stories of stymied desire, hour after hour of scheme and kill, each murder more gruesome, honed. I take notes, stick in a shiv to see if he's done, plot that he comes to a similar bad end. I shape loaves like alibis, knife-notched before they go into the oven, frenzied jabs and slices. I sharpen the blade, ready for his return. Like him, I'll never speak without a lawyer present.

Brian Harman

Slather

Knives cut
both bread and throats,
when I look past your eyes,
grab the handle,
you are already stabbed
and cooked deep
from previous trips to butchers
and bakers, I'm just
the candlestick maker, baby,
no slicing any of you,
only want to light your way,
wax poetic against the walls,
dinner with a flicker
and shadow dance, drip
down our time spent,
strip and breadsticks
for the purpose of eating,
I know how to dip
my wick and I know
how to use a knife,
but I would rather lather
with it, not cut,
but coat your throat
with my name, spread it
across your artisan skin
like warm butter,
melt and cool
to the shape of your
Machete
curves,

you
ahead
of me,
sealed,
scented,
sloppy,
slathered.

Stephen Howarth

A Vampirical Sonnet

Shall I compare thee to a blade of steel?
Thou art both softer and more adamant.
Thy touch so fairy, yet intent so real:
My virgin throat, thy object, aspirant.

Thou might kill or grant me life unending.
Adoring, I accept thy hungry kiss.
Come, my love, with wine and bread ascending—
and cutting flesh, let us share blood of bliss.

I never see thee in the light of day,
nor in the mirror's glass dost thou appear;
but to mine eyes thou art the perfect way,
and to my lips, a sense and taste most dear.

My love, I will not, cannot thee deny.
Take me for thine. Or leave us both, to die.

Sean Kelbley

Explanation

Oma's farm lay flat beside a glass-green river,
30 miles from Toledo. She said it looked like home.
And where was home? It was the summer
that my parents needed time alone. *Batschka*,
Oma said, and ran her palms across her face
as if to smooth a map. At the center of the map,
her eyes burned like specific villages.

By morning, they were light suffused through
balsam needles. Oma said, *I had two brothers,
little brothers. The army take them. Lose them.*
She sliced the warm brown bread with her specific
slicing knife, blade set parallel to wooden handle
like a violinist's bow. She buttered slices with
her rounded buttering knife. But for paprikash,

a chicken had to die. She caught the rooster
that had chased and pecked me, bound his talons,
hung him from a low branch in the dooryard,
upside-down. Slit his throat—this with a knife
I'd never seen. *Some times are bad*, she said.
Her eyes went dark and far away. *Neighbors bad.
Russians bad.* Then she turned

and smiled at me, and wiped the killing knife
across the daisies on her apron, and went inside
to put it in its special place. It was the day my
parents came to take me back. I watched the rooster
spurt and drain. We ate him and drove home.
In September, teacher said I had to use a real
country for "My Family Tree." Mom said

Hungary. Dad said Yugoslavia, but by then
it wasn't real, either, anymore. Teacher said
Put Germany. It's what she spoke. But I put
Batschka. Blood-red Magic Marker.
There are knives for slicing bread, for buttering,
for slitting throats—each knife specific
to its purpose. Anyway, you asked me

how I choose my words.

"Explanation" by Sean Kelbley was first published by *Up North Lit,* Summer 2019.

Judy Kronenfeld

My Uncle of Alcohol

Knives cut both bread and throats.

In the ancient photo speckled like
an egg, my mom's kid brother poses
on the park steps in uniform, her arm formal
in the crook of his (the dad I've barely met
is still at war). And I, at two, in ringlets,
gaze up at him. Like a bird, I took bread
at his hand. He fed me in the nest.
He read my baby cheeps and praised
inordinately. His cheeks were smooth
as knives through butter, and smelled sweetly
of Old Spice. He told the kind of stories
mothers tell, who think their sons
precocious Solomons. "My niece is brilliant,"
he'd grin. "She says, 'I have eyes,
here, in the back of my head!'"

All my years at school, he staged
puppet shows and circus acts for birthdays;
he was the judicious audience
for new clothes, and every essay
I wrote. And when he was
in his cups, my abstemious mother
never even tsk-tsked,
but whispered about the crushing wound
to his head, courtesy France '44.
She didn't say he was drunk
when the army jeep rolled over.

Comes that night (I've been living
on my own for years) when,
red as the label on the Johnny Walker
he's poured down his throat, my uncle screams
"WOMEN ARE FILTHY" and throws his wife out
with her clothes. The night when she runs
to my rooms to hide, saying, as she shakes,
he's shattered the empty bottle
in the tub.

Comes the next week (my aunt's been back
for days) he turns up at my door, whiskey-laced, and turns
on me, turns on me with anything he's got,
says I should have sought out
"an alternative," and not sent my "saintly mother"
under the knife that excised her swollen thyroid
weeks before, says his nephew Albert is the one to find
"the perfect specialist, because what do *you* know,
you idiot, you *girrrl*," and he becomes the knife thrower
and I the target *girrrl*, throat bared—
motionless with fear—whom he wants to nick
or cut or impale or scare, in whose heart
he wants to turn the serrated knife
of his contempt.

The next month he calls to invite me
to dinner, all is forgotten,
status quo ante. "How's my favorite niece?"
he says, innocent as bread.
And I, of the too many eyes, wingless,
wish I could forget.

Juliet Latham

Instructions for Cutting

Knives cut both bread and
throats but it's key to know
what knife to use
for which purpose.
I've always had a block
around knife facts.
So many lovers, gently
taking over the task
due to my bad choices:
steak knife reducing
salmon to mush,
carving knife gashing
a jelly sandwich: overkill.
Once, for my birthday,
I received a Santoku knife,
known for its three virtues:
slicing
dicing
mincing
and a gift certificate for a class
on knife skills. As always,
I didn't know
the right thing to say.
The final rift there
may have been opening
the handwritten letters
outlining her miseries
with her expensive paring knife.
In my defense, it was small
and sharp

and sliced the contents
into shards after reading.
I know this makes me
seem heartless. That knife
was a Wusthof paring knife
meant to hull strawberries,
carve soft fruits.
When it was over,
the dull blade left her
no choice but to bite
fruit whole, spit
what was unwanted.
Lately, I've taken up
tourniquet making
in the event I need
to stop blood flow
to a wound. It's
a slow process.
I've been using the
kitchen cleaver to slice
bed linens into strips.
I'm aware my method
is inefficient, my technique
irregular. If only I knew
a way to stop reaching
for the closest sharp edge
and whittle a thing
into shreds. If only I knew
how to save a thing
after I've mangled
what I love. Evenings,
I sit alone with what little
I've learned of virtue,
carving oranges

with a fillet knife,
taking care to cut only
surface deep. Inside:
a brain of thick-skinned
sections: perfectly distinct,
yet so tenderly
bound together.

Lorette C. Luzajic

Love, God, Murder

1. Rusty and mean, like running headlong into barbed wire, August comes around again.

2. *The man comes around.*

3. "Sony had the idea for three different theme albums— *Johnny Cash Sings Love Songs, Johnny Cash Sings Gospel,* and *Johnny Cash Sings Prison Songs.* I thought that was pretty cluttered, so I told them, 'How about calling the albums *Love, God and Murder*? Cut right to the chase.'" – Johnny Cash, interview with Richard Skanse, 2000, *Rolling Stone Magazine*

4. When my father went into the hospice, he left everything behind. He was finished and he knew it. He had long finished packing. He took only his black leather Bible, and a stack of Cash on CD.

5. It has been one year since I have seen my father. I still don't know how I get up each day. But I have now, hundreds of times.

6. What does prayer sound like, what does it look like? It sounds like silence. It sounds like a scream. It looks like a half empty mass shared with a few nuns at a desert church in Mexico. It is a flock of birds. It feels like Sunday morning, coming down.

7. *He's not gone,* says some well-meaning flake on the bus. *He's still with us.* Love and light and all those empty

platitudes. I see my fist smashing into his face, see him splattering like Jackson Pollock across the pleather upholstery. It's getting to my stop that saves him. I walk away, thinking, *if he's still here, then why is he not here?*

8. *The secret things belong to God, but all that is revealed to us is ours.* Deuteronomy 29:29

9. One Christmas, I gave Dad a 19 hour recording of Johnny Cash reading the New Testament. He listened to it in its entirety. He followed along.

10. When I was young, four skinheads raped and murdered my friend when she went to Toronto for a protest against sexism. I didn't know until my gas station manager slapped the *Toronto Sun* down on the desk with his double double, and her smiling face lit up the headlines on the front page. She was seventeen years old. Later, they found Brian, too, in the red company van. Picture of his family on his lap, his tie strung tight from the rearview mirror.

11. *I hung my head.*

12. I stopped believing for a long time.

13. Dad sometimes sent me a Cash album for Christmas, or Christmas in July. He gave me his hymns, and the gospel duets. I gave him the Nine Inch Nails and Leonard Cohen covers. Once when I was feeling ornery, or lost, I sent Dad a sketch I'd done in the dark, of Johnny, with graffiti scrawls of those three words. *God, love, murder*, he wrote back. *These things most often go together.*

14. The whole family stayed on one floor of the Sarnia motel

after Daddy's funeral, and it was kind of like his wedding, except the grandkids were high on wine instead of cookies and Pez.

15. When do you come to terms with love, God, murder? Face to face with any of the above, I ran screaming. I'm still running.

16. Is the pen mightier than the sword? Who said it? *A knife slices both bread and throats.*

17. Dad said he was going to write my biography one day, after he retired. It would start with Elaine, who never consented to burning out instead of fading away. It would include Crad, the writer, whom I accompanied through that shadow valley. It would talk about losing Dimitri, and Japey, and Marko, and Bobby, and Zoe, and Andy. Dad knew the title before he started: *My Daughter: a Life of Death.*

18. *You're not doing that, Dad,* I told him. But the stories keep bleeding through the cracks with the daisies.

Betsy Mars

Duality

Knives cut both bread and throats.
Fork tines tickle at your spine;
the spoon slips, nestles
into the soft bowl
of your solar plexus.

The stainless surface glints
like the ring you wear
that scratches at the throat
of your finger; your spine
straightens, you face
a fork, frost at your feet,

silver spoon of a moon
spinning possibility, rising
in the yeast, a golden boule,
a wafer on your tongue, dissolving
in the warm mouth of redemption.

Michael Minassian

The Paper Cut of Dreams

Inside a long-neglected journal
I found a letter
from an old girl friend
asking *why don't you try to find me?*

To be honest, I wasn't looking,
remembering the last time I saw her
driving away from my apartment—

she was always the most eloquent
when she spoke the language of departing
saying goodbye seemed to bring out
the best in her, a family tradition, she said.

Deciding it was best
not to poke a stick into that dream,
I read the poems I had written
many years before, preferring
the soft edges of the book,
secret and hidden messages,
backwards writing
or invisible ink I had created
with baking soda, lemon
juice, even my own urine,
the catastrophe of the everyday,
the marginalia of life.

Recalling an old proverb
my neighbor once told me:
*words, like knives, cut
both throats and bread.*

Penelope Moffet

Goat

The end of Ramadan,
the fasting over, time

to slice bread, slit
the throats of goats.

From the backseat of our car
moving through Lagos streets

a glimpse of men
in lantern light

surrounding a small creature
meant for the knife.

Darkness everywhere
except inside the circle.

Flash of white teeth,
someone staring in at me.

The heat, the flies
lifting with the sun gone

as if a pressing hand
has been removed.

We drive past as quickly
as the crowd allows.

A rope around its neck,
its four legs splayed,

the goat cries out in terror
as they drag it.

I am small, too,
and easily caught.

Robbi Nester

Uses of the Knife: Dario Cecchini

After an episode of Netflix's series The Chef's Table

We're told the pen is mightier than instruments
of war, but a pen can doom a multitude.
The knife too cuts both ways—both bread and throats.

Dario Cecchini, the world's most famous
butcher, feeds the body and the spirit,
reciting Dante and singing arias
as he carries sizzling platters
from the fire. He never thought
he'd wield the cleaver as his family
had for generations, wanting
only to stand among the cattle
in the winter fields, to heal,
and not to kill. His father's death
forced Dario from school to follow
the family craft. There he learned
to channel proper reverence
for the lives he took, to honor
those who raised the animals,
to teach the uses of the ears,
the tail, the tongue, the parts
that no one thinks to eat but those
who must and butchers, masters
of the knife, bringing life to all they serve.

Cristina M. R. Norcross

These Lines Draw Mountains

What will be your offering?
This slice of truth—
your being—
is everything you can imagine
and more than you can behold.
What lingers, like honeysuckle,
is the most you could be for someone—
and also the least.
To be the most
is to hold out bread with both hands—
an outward insistence
that someone else should go first.
Someone else can take those first petals
and scatter them on an eager bed of grass.
Knives cut both bread and throats.
Your only choice
is to let go of pride and need.
Our only hope is for all hands
to become bowls
for the dreams of others.
Release the needs of ego
in exchange for the
floating red balloon.
It holds clean air—
it holds your highest good.
Your palms have lines
that tell stories.
I am counting on those lines
to draw vast mountains.

Shannon Phillips

Black Lace Surrender

Knives cut both bread and throats.

I remember
the first time
he called me
beautiful.

It was after dinner,
in the car,
the darker backseat,
my head in his lap,
a bra strap down
a shoulder,
my neck on offer.

He said it like a curse,
like *fuck*
caged behind
gritted teeth,

like he didn't want
to admit it,
didn't want
to believe it,
didn't want
to accept the truth of our skin,

said it like he'd lost.

I wondered if later

he'd punish me,

but that night,
I chose to hear
a blessing
in a growl.

Jeannie E. Roberts

He Pleads the Fifth

Where fascicles spark and seed cones sizzle,
boughs blaze as heat lifts.

Before them, oxygen burns in smoky purple,
turns in breaths

of turquoise, circles in fumes of burgundy
and blue. Here, energy's aura emanates

from deeper regions, resounds in color
as it rushes from center of neck at level

of throat. Between them, bread and wine,
cheese, a table of offerings, where knife

shares its own reflection. Like scalpel,
her truth incises with vocal precision,

though his hides behind palings of silence.
In self-imposed choke hold, the pallid drone

of secrecy sits beside the vivid voice
of Vishuddha. Knives cut both bread and throats.

Sarah Russell

Bread and Throats

Knives cut both bread and throats,
and what woman, on occasion, slicing
a fresh baked loaf, fragrant in a kitchen warm
as an old sweater, when a husband invades
from work with a self too big, too important,
too other to slow for the aroma of afternoon labor,
arms flour-powdered and tired from kneading,
and him so rushed and out of step with kitchen pace
and peace, what woman has not looked at that knife
and thought about the difference in texture between bread
and throat, prickly with 5pm bristle, a slice through skin
more firm than the chicken she deboned for dinner, the pesky
sinew, hitting bone, searching for the notch between vertebrae.

Kenneth Salzmann

If This Be Progress (An Acrostic)

But our beginnings never know our ends!
–T.S. Eliot

Keep expectations in check when celebrating *progress* because
Nothing is ever as simple as it seems—
In humankind's urgent, stumbling dance through the
Vast gulf separating intention from effect
Every advance that moves us toward the light
Secretly contains its own shadow as well.

Consider the marvel of rockets that like knives cut through
Universes to satisfy our endless hunger for discovery,
Though more often rain death upon the Earth.

Both our capacity to build and our impulse to destroy
Originate in the very same creative drive
That might turn field grains into bread or might
Hold the seeds of our demise.

Beware, then, each steadfast conviction
Resting on a fragile hope that the
Ends we seek will be the ends we realize,
As untold numbers of poets have cautioned.
Don't assume that the wisdom and honor of science

And philosophy will save us from the folly within.
Nature or god or chance, after all, planted in our throats
Deep cries of anguish and lilting song alike.

That said, it remains ours to resist enveloping darkness,
Holding fast to knowing good likewise counterbalances bad,
Rather in the way menacing implements
Of tempered steel
Are used in times of domesticity
To carefully slice a fresh-baked loaf
Set lovingly upon the table.

Jeff Santosuossa

Double-Edged

Knives cut both bread and throats,
crust and flesh,
crumbs and blood,
drop and drip,
assorted and collected,
stainless and staining,
attracting insects and sharks.

Pens write love letters, Dear Johns—
and an occasional manifesto—
clutched to the breast, dropped impotently,
sniffed for fragrance, tear-stained,
kept forever, kept forever,
keepsake, immutable truth.

Oh, and the occasional uprising
for bread, for throats
with knives, guns, rocks
and Molotovs
formerly posted on a doorframe
later discussed stealthily,
now viral, dark-webbed
for unity, for division
peace and calm, anger and violence.

Ryan Stone

The Blade Itself

Knives cut both bread
and throats,
                       savoring
butter's slick slide
no more,
                       no less,
than the coppersnake tang
      of life
departing hot.

Honed to slash two
        from one,
to make unwhole
what once was.
           Whetted
sharp as a parent's slap,
           or a callused hand
                    at 3am,
        slicing
between pink sheets.

Brent Terry

Assassin

The poet said, *Knives cut both bread and throats,*
but I'm pretty sure he didn't mean the same knife,
since an assassin doesn't have the time, let alone
the dry cleaning budget, to go sawing away
at some poor slob's neck with a bread knife,
blood geysering over his linen trousers and Italian
calfskin loafers, victim gurgling pitifully, sirens howling
in the distance, just as the old guy behind the counter
at the sandwich shop with the Rhode Island accent
chooses a different blade when slicing a fresh loaf
of crusty pumpernickel than when shaving thin roast
beef from the bone, a third for spreading the mustard,
a fourth to neatly section fat pickles into spears,
because there is a correct job for every tool,
as my grandfather used to say, and being a barber,
he knew of what he spoke, he with his drawer
full of gleaming scissors and straight razors, which
come to think of it would be perfect for slitting throats,
but lousy for carving thick slices of rye or spiral cutting
a ham, and the right tool for cutting me
free from the depressive brambles of my nightmares
turns out this morning to be a tiger lily,
or rather, tens of thousands of tiger lillies,
which bloomed as if on cue today, exploding in vast
constellations, entire galaxies of molten orange
stars along every roadside from Willimantic
to Rockfall, along the dirt roads on which I run
my morning ten, their fire burning away—at least
for a moment—the sadness which has clung
for months like a greasy fog, and which, with the first

newscast or Facebook post will no doubt return,
but for now the sharp blades of a million petals
have excised the fat nodes of grief from my thorax,
the taut weight from the back of my throat
and I can't help but imagine how lovely the thin, green
vase would look on my living room table, displaying
but a single stem, three perfect blooms,
and I imagine, with a swift shiver of something like pain,
the quick, precisely angled cut of the pruning scissors
I inherited from my grandmother, the lillies
bending their slender necks in the breeze,
offering their throats to the blade.

Alexandra Umlas

Knife Sonnet

I heard him say *knives cut both bread and throats*—
the paradox of sharp, stabilized steel
that's used to slice so much, the apple peel,
my finger making dinner, lines on boats,
the plated steak, glued envelopes with notes,
a pie. Sometimes I carry one to feel
safer on walks, and when I portion heel
from loaf serrated blade gets all my votes.
We hardly give the credit that it's due,
and scarcely think about it when we carve
the turkey, halve the bagel, we might starve
without its magic that makes one thing two,
severs, releases, undoes, draws apart—
always has dividing at its heart.

Alan Walowitz

The Impalement Arts

The human target is the essential distinguishing feature of the impalement arts. —Wikipedia

A knife can cut bread—
or a throat, I suppose, and almost as easy,
though surely neither to be taken lightly—
not sundown the sabbath stranded near Goa on the Indian Sea—
nor on a deserted tarmac in the Kharan,
the executioner hooded like the eye of a Poe-villain,
victim since birth of one unfortunate circumstance after another.

But who would deny a knife's right
to seek another path, its own—
perhaps to dance?
To find its spotlight at the Moulin Rouge,
some latter-day Toulouse to capture all its bladed glory,
dangerous and pleased with itself
among so many brocaded sighs.

Or might it merrily prance
far from the limelight
like the Bard of Rutherford, old Dr. Williams,
front of his mirror in the north-most room,
naked, the yellow shades drawn,
and reeking loneliness—if not quite earned,
then devoutly enough wished.

But sometimes we are already more than our fondest wish—
happy enough here in the hand of the Great Throwdini
ready to be launched so near the throat

of the half-clad Target Girl, who seems not to worry
despite her sharpened skill to yelp on demand—
no more concerned who's counting the house,
than her own broken promise to bring home bread for dinner.

Julie Weiss

Poetry Class, Circa 1998
    –For Virginia

A knife cuts both bread and throats,
I write, pleased by the opening:
a scatter of bread crumbs, a splash
of blood. A crusty French baguette

which will likely remain halved
like a mouth startled open, cold cuts
sprawled in the fridge, festering.
But whose blood has spilled?

Is it a real murder or an image
of a suppressed emotion sprung
against the wall, like a moth
diving, heedless, into a light bulb?

I have only just begun, and I know
what she'll say about the mixed
metaphor, how a moth would fare better
in a forest, or as a symbol of

transformation. About the sheer lack
of a storyline. My boundless obsession
with poetic devices. Or she might not say
anything. She's been known to take

her pencil from her ear and lay it before her,
as if mourning a poem's untimely passing.
But I can't help it. I'm a frog in a pond
of words, hopping from sparkle to glow.

I want to write the line that would
set "wow" aflame. What I really want
is to wow her, to soar atop her praise
in those rare moments she's stirred.

There I've gone again, concocting
a hodgepodge of sandwiches, light bulbs,
frogs, fire, and birds, and I still don't know
whose throat was cut or why the bread's

silence speaks of stones hardened under
time's glare. Maybe this poem aims to
kill itself, and I'm wearing it as a disguise.
"Say what you mean!" That familiar bear roar

echoing across mountains, quaking my
dreams, entire stanzas slashed and bleeding
and yet I come back for more,
the bones of old poems heaped on the desk

I take next to hers. Twenty years from now
when my poetry is no longer soaked in
language, I'll wriggle out of my ego and sling
my voice backwards across the years to say:

"you were right. You were always right.
I was just too callow to know." But it's still
1998. I am sitting in her classroom,
head bowed, scrawling notes in the margins

of my latest work, silently defending my
moth, which does, in fact, represent death
in some European cultures. As she sighs

her thousandth sigh, I am thinking:

if cold cuts can exhale their last breath
and an emotion can grow matter enough
to spatter against a surface, what need have I
to justify a piece of bread and a throat?

Acknowledgements

First and foremost, my appreciation goes to Marc Di Martino who generously gifted me this line to do with what I would. It was so evocative and inspired such wide-ranging responses. This project has provided me with so much reading pleasure and deepened connections with the poets who contributed to this, my first publishing venture. I am honored that they have entrusted me with their work.

I absolutely could not have pulled this off without the help of Shannon Phillips who has patiently taught me the ropes (or at least concealed her impatience). I am a bit of a techno-dinosaur, and part of what was great about this undertaking was proving to myself that I could undertake new challenges, albeit with a lot of handholding. She is a saint and a magician.

To Lorette Luzajic for working with me and tolerating my indecisiveness about the direction of the artwork, alternating with my puny attempts at micromanagement. She is a genius at her crafts and I am beyond grateful to have her work grace the cover, as well as her heart-wrenching poem.

My friends and family have been supportive of the time and energy I have invested, and I am indebted to my daughter, Kat Naphas, who designed my press logo and provided other aesthetic guidance. I have always had faith in her creative abilities, and it has been a joy to work with her. My son, Daniel Naphas, has a special talent for scrupulous attention to detail, and I am grateful for his willingness to tackle this manuscript to ensure uniformity and accuracy. My father would be proud to have been the progenitor of this line of bibliophiles and anal editors.

Lastly, despite my love-hate relationship with social media, I would not know virtually any of these poets had it not been for Facebook. The breadth and depth of relationships that I have gained cannot be overestimated. Just look at where these poets reside to get a sense of the global poetic community that has emerged via this platform. In this case, I hope the medium is not the message.

Biographies

Jay Brecker lives and works in Southern California. He is a field-hand of workshops and extension classes. His work will have or has appeared in *I-70 Review, RHINO Poetry, New Mexico Review, OVS Magazine, Bird's Thumb* and a chapbook, *[dialog box]*, from Thistle and Weed Press, 2012.

Marc Alan Di Martino was born and raised on the East Coast of the United States and attended Virginia Commonwealth University, majoring in visual arts. After college he moved to New York City, where he spent eight years working in the city's best used bookshops, collecting vinyl and gathering material for future use. He moved to Italy in 2003, where he now lives with his family. His poetry has appeared in *Rattle, Baltimore Review, The New Yorker, Palette Poetry* and many other places, including the anthology *What Remains: The Many Ways We Say Goodbye*. His first collection, *Unburial*, will be released by Kelsay Books in 2020. He can be found at www.marcalandimartino.com.

Alexis Rhone Fancher is published in *Best American Poetry 2016, Rattle, Hobart, Verse Daily, Plume, Tinderbox, Cleaver, Diode, SWWIM, The MacGuffin, Nasty Women Poets, Nashville Review, Rust + Moth, decomP, Duende,* and elsewhere. She's authored five collections, most recently *The Dead Kid Poems* (KYSO Flash, 2019). Her latest collection, *EROTIC: New & Selected,* publishes in 2020 from New York Quarterly. A multiple Pushcart Prize and Best of the Net nominee, Alexis is poetry editor of *Cultural Weekly*. www.alexisrhonefancher.com

Brian Harman received his MFA in Creative Writing from Cal State University, Long Beach. His poems have appeared in *Chiron Review, Nerve Cowboy, Redshift, Vamp Cat Magazine, V: An Anthology,* and elsewhere. He loves craft beer, creating music playlists, writing poetry past midnight, and is proud to represent his hometown of Yorba Linda, CA.

Stephen Howarth was born and raised in England, but, being half-Shetland, he has poetry in his blood. He sometimes sports a top hat bought in Whitby, North Yorkshire, where even the young Goths admired it. He hasn't visited Transylvania.

Sean Kelbley began submitting poetry for publication in 2017. Since then, his poetry has appeared on the nature trails of The Ridges at Ohio University; in Athens (Ohio) Poet Laureate Kari Gunter-Seymour's curated anthology *Essentially Athens;* and at a number of other fine places including *Crab Creek Review, New Verse News, One* (Jacar Press), *Rattle, Poets Reading the News,* and *Up North Lit*. His work been recognized in contests at *Midwest Review, Still: The Journal,* and the Yuki Teikei Haiku Society, and his first published poem, "True Story," was nominated by *Rise Up Review* for 2017 Best of the Net. Sean lives with his husband on a 330-acre farm in southeastern Ohio, in a house they built themselves. He works as an elementary school counselor.

Judy Kronenfeld is the author of four full-length collections and two chapbooks of poetry, including *Bird Flying through the Banquet* (FutureCycle, 2017), *Shimmer* (WordTech, 2012), and *Light Lowering in Diminished Sevenths*, 2nd edition (Antrim House, 2012)—winner of the 2007 Litchfield Review Poetry Book Prize. Her poems have appeared in *Cider Press Review, Cimarron Review, Connotation Press, DMQ Review, Ghost Town, Miramar, Natural Bridge, One (Jacar Press), Rattle, Valparaiso Poetry Review,* and other journals, and in two dozen anthologies. Her creative nonfiction has appeared nine times in *Under the Sun* and has also been published in *Hippocampus* and *Inlandia: A Literary Journey,* among other places. She is Lecturer Emerita, Creative Writing Department, University of California, Riverside, and an Associate Editor of the online poetry journal, *Poemeleon*.

Juliet Latham lives in West Chester, PA, where she is a full-time corporate trainer. She holds a master's degree in creative writing and taught writing for 10 years at Temple University in Philadelphia. Her work has been published in a variety of places, including *Rattle, The Ekphrastic Review, The Journal, Eleven Eleven, Boxcar Poetry Review, Pindeldyboz,* and *Nine Muses Poetry*.

Lorette C. Luzajic is an artist and writer from Toronto, Ontario. Her mixed media collage paintings are collected around the world, and she often writes about art. She is the founder and editor of *The Ekphrastic Review*.
Visit her at www.mixedupmedia.ca.

Betsy Mars is a Connecticut-born, mostly California-raised poet and educator. She has two degrees from the University of Southern California which she puts to no obvious use. Her work has recently appeared or is upcoming in *The Blue Nib*, *One Sentence Poems*, and *Shiela-Na-Gig*. Her photography has been published in several journals, most recently in *Rattle*, where her photo was chosen as the ekphrastic prompt for March 2019. Her first chapbook, *Alinea*, (Picture Show Press) was published in January 2019. 2019 reminded her that life is full of the unexpected, for better and for worse.

Michael Minassian: The poet claims not to exist and has written several obituaries, none of them true. Whenever he hears a birdsong, he barks like a dog. In summer, he fries eggs on the sidewalk, opens hydrants with a toothbrush, and claims drowned sailors visit him at inappropriate moments. His work has appeared in several publications, some in slightly different form, some not at all. For more information: www.michaelminassian.com

Penelope Moffet is the author of two chapbooks of poetry, *It Isn't That They Mean to Kill You* (Arroyo Seco Press, 2018) and *Keeping Still* (Dorland Mountain Arts Colony, 1995). Her poems have appeared in many literary journals, including *Natural Bridge*, *Permafrost*, *Levure Litteraire*, *Pearl*, *The Rise Up Review*, *The Sow's Ear Poetry Review*, *The Ekphrastic Review* and *The Missouri Review*. Her poems have also been published in *Coiled Serpent: Poets Arising from the Cultural Quakes and Shifts of Los Angeles* (Tia Chucha Press, 2016) and *what wildness is this: Women Write about the Southwest* (University of Texas Press, 2007). A former freelance journalist and editor, for the last 22 years she has earned her living as a legal secretary.

Robbi Nester is the author of four books of poetry. She is completing work on a fifth, a chapbook of poems about chefs tentatively entitled *Plated*. Her poems, reviews, essays, and blog posts have appeared widely.

Shannon Phillips earned her MFA in creative writing from California State University, Long Beach. She is the co-founder of the annual Mother's Day poetry reading at Gatsby Books and the recipient of the 28th Moon Prize from *Writing In A Woman's Voice*. Her most recent chapbook, *Bedroom Poems*, is available from Small Fish Big Pond.

Cristina M. R. Norcross is the editor of the online poetry journal, *Blue Heron Review (www.blueheronreview.com)*, and the author of 8 poetry collections. Her latest book is *Beauty in the Broken Places* (Kelsay Books, 2019). Cristina's poems have been published, or are forthcoming, in: *The Toronto Quarterly, Visual Verse, Your Daily Poem,* and *Pirene's Fountain*, among others. Cristina is the co-founder of Random Acts of Poetry and Art Day (celebrated annually on Feb. 20th). Find out more about this author at: www.cristinanorcross.com

Jeannie E. Roberts has authored six books, including *The Wingspan of Things* (Dancing Girl Press, 2017), *Romp and Ceremony* (Finishing Line Press, 2017), *Beyond Bulrush* (Lit Fest Press, 2015), and *Nature of it All* (Finishing Line Press, 2013). Her work appears in print and online in North American and international journals and anthologies. She is poetry editor of the online literary magazine *Halfway Down the Stairs*. When she's not reading, writing, or editing, you can find her drawing and painting, or outdoors photographing her natural surroundings.

Sarah Russell's poetry and fiction have been published in *Kentucky Review, Red River Review, Misfit Magazine, Rusty Truck, Third Wednesday*, and many other journals and anthologies. She is a Pushcart Prize nominee, and her poetry collection *I lost summer somewhere* was published in 2019 by Kelsay Books. She blogs at www.sarahrussellpoetry.net.

Kenneth Salzmann's poems appear in numerous print and online journals and anthologies. His recent book, *The Last Jazz Fan and Other Poems*, is available from Amazon. He lives in Mexico's Sierra Madre mountains with his wife, two rescued dogs, and his *tarjeta de verde*.

Jeff Santosuosso is a business consultant and award-winning poet living in Pensacola, FL. His chap book, *Body of Water*, is available through Clare Songbirds Publishing House. He is Editor-in-Chief of www.*panoplyzine.com*, an online journal of poetry and short prose. Jeff's work has been nominated for the Pushcart Prize and has appeared in *San Pedro River Review, South Florida Poetry Journal, Mojave Desert Review, The Lake (UK), Red Fez, First Literary Review-East, Texas Poetry Calendar, Avocet,* and other online and print publications.

Ryan Stone writes after midnight in Melbourne, Australia. He lives beside Sherbrooke Forest with his wife, two young sons, a German Shepherd, and a rag doll cat. On daily walks through his sylvan surrounds, he often falls down rabbit holes.

Brent Terry's poems, stories, plays, essays and reviews have appeared in dozens of magazines. He is the author of the poetry collections *yesnomaybe*, *Wicked*, *Excellently*, and the recently released *Troubadour Logic*, as well as a forthcoming novel, *The Body Electric*. Among the honors he has garnered are a fellowship from the Connecticut Arts and Tourism Board and the 2017 Connecticut Poetry Prize, as well as nominations for *Best of the Net* and *Bettering American Poetry*. Terry has worked with writers of all ages and abilities, and currently teaches creative writing and literature at Eastern Connecticut State University. He lives in and runs the trails around Willimantic, CT.

Alexandra Umlas is the author of the poetry collection *At the Table of the Unknown* (Moon Tide Press). She serves as a reader for *Palette Poetry* and on the board of directors of Tebot Bach, a non-profit literary organization. She is a recent graduate of Cal State University of Long Beach's MFA Poetry program and currently lives in Huntington Beach, CA with her husband and two daughters. www.alexandraumlas.com

Alan Walowitz was a teacher of secondary English for 34 years, mostly in New York City public schools. He served as the Coordinator of English Language Arts in White Plains, NY Public Schools from 1992 till 2004. For the last 15 years, he's taught at Manhattanville College in Westchester. Alan's poems have been nominated for a Pushcart Prize in 2017 and 2018. He's a Contributing Editor at *Verse-Virtual,* an Online Community Journal of Poetry. His chapbook, *Exactly Like Love* was published by Osedax Press. His full-length book, *The Story of the Milkman and Other Poems*, is available from Truth Serum Press.

Julie Weiss received her BA in English Literature and Creative Writing from San Jose State University. She's a 44-year-old ex-pat from Foster City, California who moved to Spain in 2001 and never looked back. She works as a telephone English teacher from her home in Guadalajara, where she lives with her wife, 4-year-old daughter, and 1-year-old son. Her work appears in *Lavender Review, Sinister Wisdom, The American Journal of Poetry, Santa Clara Review,* and *Sky Island Journal,* among others. You can find her on Twitter @colourofpoetry or on her website at www.julieweiss2001.wordpress.com

www.ingramcontent.com/pod-product-compliance
Lightning Source LLC
Chambersburg PA
CBHW031430040426
42444CB00006B/762